"The Lives of Faith and Grace series will not only engage the minds, hearts, and imaginations of middle grade readers, it will also offer examples of heroes worth emulating. These true stories will challenge our youth to live courageously for the name of Jesus and see the joy and privilege it is to be a part of something far bigger than themselves."

Sarah Walton, coauthor, *Hope When It Hurts*; author, *The Long Road Home*

"This is a remarkable series of biographies about Christian leaders our children should know. Beautifully written and illustrated, these stories help nurture the faith of the next generation by illuminating the stories of God's faithfulness among that great cloud of witnesses in heaven. You'll want all these books for your home, church, or school library."

Daniel Darling, Director of The Land Center for Cultural Engagement, Southwestern Baptist Theological Seminary; author, *The Characters of Christmas* and *The Characters of Easter*

The Story of Eric Liddell

Lives of Faith and Grace

Edited by Champ Thornton

The Story of John Bunyan: The Prisoner Who Wrote Pilgrim's Progress

The Story of Eric Liddell: The Runner Who Lived for God's Glory

The Story of Katie Luther: The Nun Who Escaped to True Freedom

The Story of Martin Luther: The Monk Who Changed the World

The Story of Corrie ten Boom: The Watchmaker Who Forgave Her Enemies

The Story of Harriet Tubman: The Trailblazer Who Led Many to Freedom

The Story of Phillis Wheatley: The African Poet Who Called America to Christ

Lives of Faith and Grace

The Story of Eric Liddell

The Runner Who Lived for God's Glory

Champ Thornton

CROSSWAY®

WHEATON, ILLINOIS

The Story of Eric Liddell: The Runner Who Lived for God's Glory

Published by Crossway
1300 Crescent Street
Wheaton, Illinois 60187

Cover and interior illustrations: T. Lively Fluharty

First printing 2026

Printed in the United States of America

All emphases in Scripture quotations have been added by the author.

Trade paperback ISBN: 978-1-4335-8345-2
ePub ISBN: 978-1-4335-8348-3
PDF ISBN: 978-1-4335-8346-9

Library of Congress Cataloging-in-Publication Data

Names: Thornton, Champ, 1973- author.
Title: The story of Eric Liddell : The Runner Who Lived for God's Glory / Champ Thornton.
Description: Wheaton, IL : Crossway, [2025] | Series: Lives of faith and grace | Includes bibliographical references. | Audience: Ages 8-13
Identifiers: LCCN 2024038311 (print) | LCCN 2024038312 (ebook) | ISBN 9781433583452 (paperback) | ISBN 9781433583469 (pdf) | ISBN 9781433583483 (epub)
Subjects: LCSH: Liddell, Eric, 1902-1945. | Rugby football players—Scotland—Biography. | LCGFT: Biographies.
Classification: LCC GV944.9.L53 T46 2025 (print) | LCC GV944.9.L53 (ebook) | DDC 796.42/2092 [B]—dc23/eng/20250203
LC record available at https://lccn.loc.gov/2024038311
LC ebook record available at https://lccn.loc.gov/2024038312

Crossway is a publishing ministry of Good News Publishers.

VP 35 34 33 32 31 30 29 28 27 26
15 14 13 12 11 10 9 8 7 6 5 4 3 2 1

For my colleagues at Crossway

—friends and colaborers in the transmission

of the treasure of the gospel—

"Let us run with endurance the race that

is set before us, looking to Jesus."

(Hebrews 12:1–2)

"Many of us are missing something in life

because we are after the second best."

ERIC LIDDELL

Contents

1

The Greatest Race

1923

IT'S SATURDAY AFTERNOON, July 14, 1923. The summer sun blazes down on the oval race track, its surface of finely crushed rock baked flat and hard. Athletes from across the British Isles—from England, Ireland, and Scotland—are gathered for a track meet in an English city called Stoke-on-Trent (a six-hour drive north of London, England).

Occasional gusts of wind ripple the thin uniforms of the six runners coming onto the track. They're getting ready for the next race: the quarter-mile. Some of the men are fresh. It's their first race of the day.

Eric Liddell has already run twice. Today, he first ran the 100-yard sprint and won. But this is no surprise. The week before he ran the 100-yard race in 9.7 seconds, setting a new British record. Eric's a natural sprinter. But this twenty-one-year-old from Scotland, whom they nicknamed the "Flying Scotsman" for his speed, wasn't done. Today he also ran the 220-yard race—that's half a lap around the track. He won again—22.3 seconds.

And now it's time for the 440-yard race, which is not his usual distance. It's one full lap, a quarter of a mile. So for the third time today, Eric walks to the starting line. He shakes hands with the other runners, and then takes his place on the inside lane next to the grassy infield. He looks down the sun-dried track, still solid but now dotted with thousands of tiny cuts. The sharp spikes of leather running shoes have started to break up the solid surface, giving it a little more traction. The runners take their marks. They get set. *Go!*

The pack surges forward. There's confusion, as runners crash into each other. Within three steps, Eric is tripped up. Pushed off the track, he's on his hands and knees in the grass.

That seems to be it.

Half a second ticks by. Eric thinks he's been disqualified. The other runners pound down the dusty track. Another second. Someone's shouting—*Eric! Get up! Run!* This race isn't over!

Eric springs to his feet and launches himself down the track. The runners are almost 20 yards ahead of him. He digs deep. With his face to the heavens, he runs like he's never run before. He gains ground with every step, leaving tiny clouds of grit behind him. Closer. Closer. Now he's at the back of the pack. He passes one runner. And then another.

Coming out of the final turn, Eric's in fourth place. He's 10 yards behind the leader, Englishman

J. J. Gillis, who had tripped him up at the beginning of the race.

Eric rips past the next runner, then the next. He's five yards behind. There's 40 yards to go in the race. Now he's two steps behind Gillis. They thunder toward the tape. Eric catches him, passes him, stretches out the lead, and flashes across the finish line, two yards ahead.

Eric Henry Liddell wins the quarter-mile in 51.1 seconds! He collapses to the ground, exhausted. The crowd goes wild.

What a comeback! What a race! No one had seen anything like it before. Some wondered if Eric surely got a little help from the wind. Others called it a miracle.

But this race showed the world what Eric Liddell could do. It also demonstrated what kind of man he was. As an athlete, Eric was dedicated to practicing hard, learning how to improve, and doing his best. Over the years, he ran in many races, some small and some big, including the Olympics. He won so often that he became one of the most famous names in Great Britain.

Yet as a Christian, Eric was also running another kind of race. "The greatest race," he would say. Throughout his life of service to God, Eric wanted to work hard, grow in godliness, and give his best. Like his running, he knew how it felt to get knocked down and to face terrible challenges. He also knew how to get up and, only in God's strength, to struggle forward and finally finish. He wasn't living for himself; he was striving to glorify someone else—the Lord.

As his friends joyously carried Eric from the track on that hot July day, few realized what obstacles he had overcome to get there. And no one could've imagined the course of life that lay before him, or how this runner's race through life would one day end.

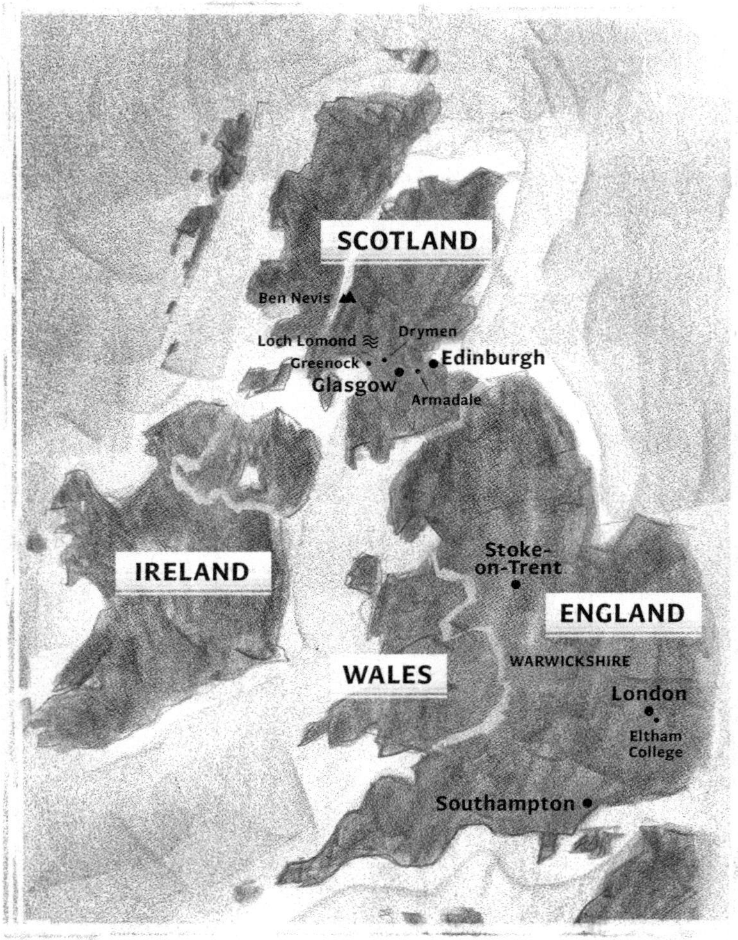

— PRONUNCIATION AID —

Drymen: DRIH-men **Edinburgh:** EH-din-Bur-row **Glasgow:** GLAZ-go

Great Britain is made up of several historically sovereign nations, such as England and Scotland, that have united under one main government based in London, but each country retains some unique independence from the others as well.

2

The Start

1902–1906

MANY PEOPLE MIGHT be surprised to discover where Eric Liddell grew up. This Scottish Olympic runner actually spent his childhood in China. Born on January 16, 1902, in Tientsin (now Tianjin), China, Eric spent most of his first six years in the small village of Siaochang (now Xiaozhang). Located on the edge of

China's Great Plains, his hometown was a forty-hour wagon ride south of the capital city of Beijing.

When a young Eric would step outside his small house each morning, he could only see high mud walls surrounding his home and three others. Beyond the gates of this missionary compound, he saw a very different scene. Open horizons lay in every direction, filled with endless brown fields of grain and thinly veiled with the smoke of cooking fires from countless huts.

Eric had bright blue eyes and blond hair, and his parents were missionaries from Scotland. But young Eric thought of himself as Chinese. That's how he dressed, how he ate, how he lived, and how he learned to speak. As a preschooler, when he couldn't catch some kittens, he screamed his first Chinese words: "*Hsieo mao pao la!*" ("Little cat has run away!") When Eric thought about home, Scotland did not come to mind.

Eric was a missionary kid. His father, James Dunlop Liddell, had grown up near the beautiful Loch

Lomond in Scotland. In 1898, engaged to a Scottish nurse named Mary Reddin, James moved to northern China to be a missionary. Not many Christians lived in that part of the country. Most Chinese men and women believed in *Buddhism*, a religion that was started five hundred years before Jesus's birth by its founder, Siddartha Gautama. Thought to have special insight, this teacher was "an awakened one" (a *Buddha*), who taught people to escape suffering by eliminating their desires and living according to certain rules.

James, as part of the London Missionary Society, had gone to China to tell people about the God-man, Jesus Christ. Jesus didn't call people to remove their desires, but to satisfy their hearts in the goodness and grace of God. He didn't tell people to earn their salvation by obeying rules, but instead to *rely* on him—the one who had earned their salvation for them. Twelve months after James had come to China, his fiancée also arrived. They were married in Shanghai, China, in 1899.

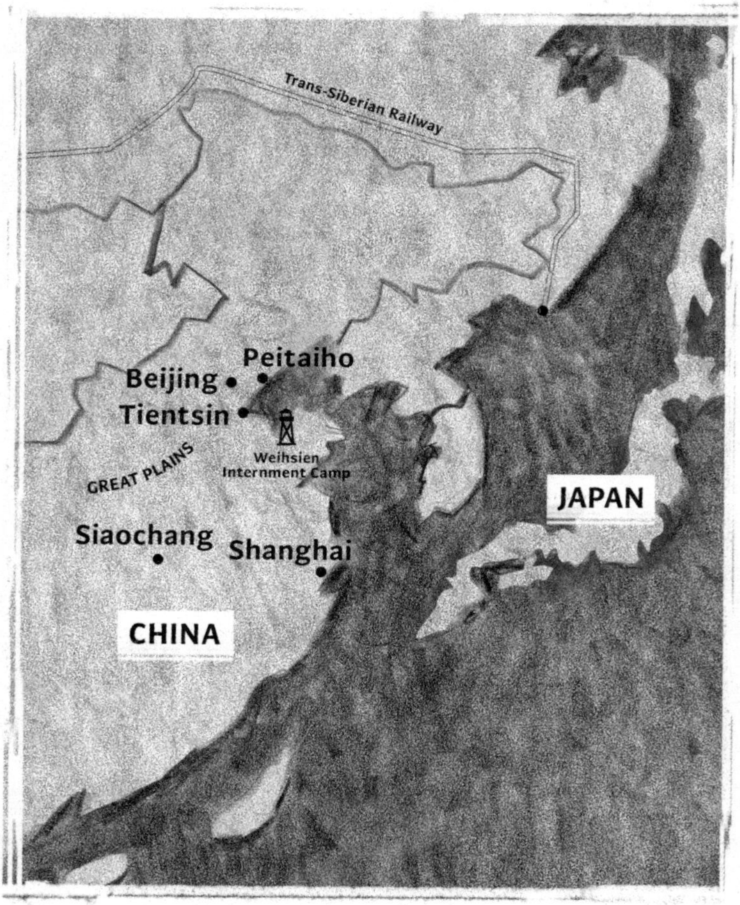

— PRONUNCIATION AID —

Beijing: bay-JING
Peitaiho: bay-die-huh
Shanghai: SHANG-high
Siaochang: SHAUW-chawng
Tientsin: tee-inZIN
Weihsien: WAY-shin

Some of the spellings and names for Chinese cities have changed since Eric's day. This map uses terms that Eric knew.

Over the next number of years, the Liddells had four children: Robert "Rob" (b. 1900), Eric (b. 1902), Jenny (b. 1903), and eventually Ernest (b. 1912). They lived inside the mission compound in the village of Siaochang. James worked hard to take care of his

— The Boxer Rebellion —

In October 1899, the same month as the Liddells' marriage, China was ripped apart by a bloody war called the Boxer Rebellion. This war was started by violent men trained in martial arts like kung fu. These "boxers" hated all the foreigners who had come to China and who seemed to be changing their country and culture. Over a hundred thousand people were killed in that war. About thirty thousand of them were Christians, and more than 250 were missionaries. For two years, James and Mary Liddell faced and survived many threats from this uprising, but in 1901 they were able to escape to a less dangerous location.

family, but sometimes his missionary work took him away for months. Thousands of tiny villages filled the vast area around Siaochang. Ten million people called this area home. So James traveled deep into the Chinese countryside, spreading the gospel and helping people. There were so many needs. And all around were robbers, floods, sickness, dangerous soldiers, and little food.

Yet through all the hardship, Eric's parents worked hard and helped people. They served others, because James and Mary were following the Lord's command and his example. And they also took care of their growing family. Each summer, they would vacation together at the beach in Peitaiho. Their mission agency owned a few wooden beach houses at this resort town. Eric and his family enjoyed games together, swimming in the cool ocean water, and long talks and walks on the shore.

Eric loved his parents. He watched them care for their family and give themselves for others. He learned a lot from his mom and dad.

Through their example, he learned to serve others, and he learned to suffer. When he was four years old, Eric became terribly sick with a serious illness. He could've died. There were no doctors nearby. So his mother did her best to help him. She gave him the medicine she had on hand. The label on the brown glass bottle announced its not very appetizing name: Valentine's Meat Juice (squeezed from pieces of raw beef).

Eventually Eric got better, but the sickness (or perhaps the medicine) had made his legs numb and lifeless. One person who saw him said he would "never be able to run again." Forget running; young Eric could hardly walk.

So for people who knew Eric Liddell as a four-year-old boy, no one would have thought, "Look at that kid! One day, he'll break British running records." The boy who would become the "Flying Scotsman" didn't grow up around sports. His parents were missionaries—not athletes. Eric faced physical challenges. His legs had been harmed by an awful disease.

And Eric lived in China. This was his home, not Scotland. While he had heard stories about the land where his parents had grown up, he had never been there.

Soon all of this was about to change.

3

First Strides

1907–1920

ERIC WAS FIVE YEARS OLD when he first walked the ancient dirt paths around his father's hometown of Drymen in central Scotland. James and Mary Liddell had come home to Scotland for a year sabbatical. It must have felt wonderful for Eric to stretch his legs in the open green countryside after having been stuck on a boat for over fifty days. The voyage from China to Great Britain through the Suez Canal is over 12,000 miles long. But Eric's journey was not yet over.

Before long he and his family were traveling again, this time by train, across 450 miles of land. The Liddells were enrolling their two sons at a boarding school for the children of missionaries, a common practice at the time. Founded to grow both knowledge and character in students, boarding schools were academies where students lived apart from their parents during the school year. Located in south London, Eltham College featured cream-colored brick buildings around a central grassy courtyard or green. (A "college," at that time, did not necessarily mean it was for older teens who had finished high school.) In Eltham's classrooms, students would learn a variety of subjects like history, literature, physics, music, drawing, algebra, trigonometry, science, and the classics.

After getting Rob and Eric set up at school, their father returned to China. But their mother and sister didn't leave until the following year. The night his mother sailed back to China, six-year-old Eric went to his dorm room, curled up on his cot, and cried himself to sleep.

For the next twelve years, Eric, along with his older brother, Rob, would call this boarding school home. They wore gray flannel school uniforms (including jackets, ties, and caps), ate some pretty awful cafeteria food, went to classes, did homework, and lived in the school dormitories.

Thousands of miles separated son from father. But Eric Liddell was reminded of his father often. The Latin motto of Eltham College—*Gloria Filiorum Patres*—means "The fathers are the glory of the sons." While Eric only saw his parents once during his years at Eltham, he adored his mother and father. When he grew up, he wanted to be a missionary like his father. Yet even as a child, Eric already tried to follow his father's example.

As Eric had seen his father do in the Chinese countryside, Eric tried to serve others. At the age of eight, when Eric saw older students bullying younger ones, he stepped in to help. He tried to stand for what was right and just, even if it got him into trouble.

One day, Eric saw someone riding a bicycle across the school green. This was against the school rules. So Eric fearlessly called out, "Hey, no cycling there!" It didn't matter to Eric that the rider of the bike was also the headmaster of the school. Right was always right, even if the results didn't turn out right. (The headmaster sent Eric to his room without his evening meal.)

Yet, as a friend said, Eric wasn't "narrow" or stuffy; instead, he had "such a big heart." When people saw him, they said Eric was an example of "Christian brotherliness." They even said he was like his father. To him this was a compliment; there was hardly a person Eric admired more than James Liddell.

Eric was also a quiet and thoughtful student. One year, in the school play, Eric had what he considered the perfect role, one with very few lines. He played the sleepy and lazy Dormouse in *Alice in Wonderland*. Eric was himself a bit shy, so this role gained him a nickname: "Mouse." Yet unlike the character in the play, Eric was certainly not lazy. In addition to attending Bible studies and church, he took classes in Latin and Greek, philosophy and science, English and history. But in school he loved learning about science most of all, especially the experiments! His teacher, A. P. Cullen, would entertain science students by reading thick textbooks like he was a performer in a play and by introducing the sights and smells of offbeat laboratory demonstrations. What could be more thrilling than taking a favorite subject and bringing it into real life where it could be seen in action?

And people also began to notice Eric himself coming to life. Although he didn't like talking to a crowd, he certainly didn't mind competing in front of them. Eric loved rugby, where he played the wing position—and with the ball, he could fly like he had wings on his feet! A friend who watched him play said, "He was a tireless and unshakable defender, and when he smother-tackled you, you stayed smothered."

— What Is Rugby? —

Rugby may have started as early as 1823. Yet the rules for this team sport were drawn up at Rugby School in Warwickshire, England in 1845.

In this winter sport two teams, each made up of fifteen players, try to score points by getting the ball into the other team's endzone. The endzones are at opposite ends of the field, similar to American football. Both rugby and football fields are around 100 yards long (rugby is 109 yards, football is 100 exactly). Like football, players may kick the ball through upright posts for extra points. Similarly, the ball for both sports is shaped like an oval (though rugby's ball is a bit bigger), and players may run with the ball and pass or throw it backward and sideways to other players. But unlike American football, rugby players may never pass or throw the ball forward toward the endzone they are trying to reach, and they do not wear protective pads.

Eric also played cricket. By the time he was fifteen years old, he was a starting player for Eltham's best rugby and cricket teams, and later he became the captain of both teams for several years. He was a gifted athlete. And so was his older brother, Rob.

Through their sports victories at Eltham in 1918, Eric and Rob caused the other students to give that year's school championship a new nickname: "The Liddell Games." Rob captured first place in the hurdles, cross-country, and the high jump competitions, and Eric won the long jump and the 440-yard race. But his best events were the shorter races. He won the 100-yard sprint in a blazing 10.8 seconds. And the next year, he cut his time down to 10.2 seconds—a new school record!

Eric graduated from Eltham in 1920. And as he grew up and grew faster, he was gaining more and more attention—and not for just his speed.

When he ran, he looked wild. "I don't remember my first view of anyone as vividly as my first sight of Eric Liddell," recalled Duncan Wright, a famous

— What Is Cricket? —

Cricket is a team sport, played in the summer, which started in the 1500s in England. Like baseball, it uses a ball and bat. Like field hockey and American football, each team has eleven players. The bowler (who acts as a pitcher) throws the ball at three wooden posts that are 28 inches tall, called *wickets*. His aim is to hit the wickets. But the batter, standing a little to the side of the wickets, tries to protect them by hitting the ball away with his paddle-shaped bat. Sometimes the batters themselves get hit, so they wear special padded uniforms, gloves, and helmet. If the batter hits the ball into the air and it's caught by an opposing team member before the ball hits the ground, the batter is out (just like in baseball). Almost every town in England has its own cricket team, and sometimes games last for several days! But that's not commonly considered a problem, since cricket is one of the most beloved sports in all of England.

marathon runner. He first saw this 5-foot, 9-inch, 154-pound athlete run at the Queen's Park Sports track not long after Eric started studying science at the University of Edinburgh.

"Through a small window from the competitor's room underneath the stand," recalled Duncan, "I saw Eric for the first run in the 100-yards and was completely thrilled. Off to a slow start, he ran with

blazing speed, chin up, head back on shoulders, and his arms thrashing the air."

During races, with his arms flailing and his head tipped back like he was looking at the sky, Eric ran like a windmill, on fire, strapped to a raging bull.

People shook their heads and snickered at his awkward style, but his race times were no joke.

And one man who watched Eric run wasn't laughing at all.

4

In Training

1920–1922

TOM MCKERCHAR, a forty-four-year-old, part-time athletic trainer, had a reputation for being serious. Employed during the week at an Edinburgh printing company, McKerchar did scientific research as a hobby to discover the best way to train athletes. Back then, lots of other trainers also had ideas.

But today we'd think they were crazy; their training ideas included smoking, drinking lots of beer, swimming in icy water, and taking strong and awful medicines.

Before meeting Tom McKerchar, Eric Liddell had his own crazy ideas about training. Once to prepare for a race, Eric and four friends cycled up the highest mountain in Scotland (Ben Nevis's peak is 4,413 feet above sea level). The 350-mile trip took six days. After getting home, Eric realized his mistake: "I was stiff, there was no spring in my muscles. Only three or four more weeks before I was to make my first appearance in public as a runner." The university didn't provide a trainer, and by now Eric knew he needed someone to help him.

Yet Eric didn't know if the serious trainer who had approached him was the right choice. At first McKerchar seemed stern and harsh. But, Eric said later, "He taught me where I was going wrong." And a man like that could help Eric. But it wasn't going to be easy.

Yet McKerchar cared about the men he trained. To him they weren't just athletes, they were people. Like other coaches, McKerchar expected his athletes to work hard and show up on time. But unlike most coaches at that time, he made them warm up before strenuous exercise, he rubbed down their tight muscles, and he evaluated his runners' form by watching slow-motion films of them running.

Eric said of his trainer: "He took me in hand, pounded me about like a piece of putty, pushed this muscle this way and that muscle the other way, in order, as he said, to get me into shape."

McKerchar also tried to fix Eric's wild running style. But it didn't work. That was just the way Eric ran. So instead, McKerchar taught Eric the basics. And day after day, Eric worked hard. All this practice was new to him. "Training is not the easiest thing to do," Eric said. It could become boring "with the continual repetition of certain exercises." And "one of the hardest lessons," Eric admitted, was just learning "how to start."

But McKerchar showed Eric how. He taught Eric how to start from a crouching position. (On old-fashioned tracks made from crushed rock, or cinders, runners would dig two small holes behind the starting line, one for each foot to give the best traction, instead of having starting blocks like runners use today.) He trained Eric to make his first step a small one—"just a foot or perhaps 18 inches"—and then steadily rise to full speed. He coached Eric on running strategy. And he showed him how to lean forward at the finish line.

Eric listened. He learned. He worked hard. And it showed.

In his first season, Eric mainly ran two race distances: the 100-yard and the 220-yard. In that first year as a student at Edinburgh University, Eric ran the 100-yard ten times and was only beaten once. He ran the 220-yard seven times, always finishing in the top four.

It didn't take people long to realize something special was going on. Crowds began to show up at Eric's races, just to watch him run.

His second season at Edinburgh was even better. In his first race, at Craiglockhart Stadium in Edinburgh, Eric set a record in the 100-yard and the 220-yard. And he also ran the 440-yard race one time and finished first! For Eric, his serious coach had

— Making the Grade —

What was Eric Liddell like as a university student? A close friend of Eric gave this description of Eric's study habits and grades at Edinburgh University:

> In 1920–21, Eric's grades were 94% in Inorganic Chemistry and 83% in Mathematics. . . . Anyone might be proud of this, and it demonstrates that Eric Liddell wasn't guilty of neglecting his studies. School wasn't a second place, even to athletics. In the Olympic year [1924] there was, it is true, a slight falling away, but his grades never fell below 68%.

by now also become "my friend," and McKerchar called Eric, "my wonderful boy."

Yet throughout his victorious second season, Eric experienced challenges as a runner. For the first three months, he won first place in almost every race. But his times weren't getting faster, and in the last month of the season he didn't even qualify for some of the final rounds.

Eric also encountered challenges off the track. After a race in Greenock, Scotland, seventy miles away from Edinburgh, Eric was riding home in the sidecar of a motorcycle. Suddenly, the connector—which held the sidecar and motorcycle together—came loose! The sidecar veered off on its own and Eric fell out and struck the ground with a hard thump. All of this was unnoticed by his friend on the motorcycle,

ERIC'S BEST TIMES DURING HIS UNIVERSITY YEARS (1921–1924)

(All times in seconds)

	100-YARD RACE	220-YARD RACE	440-YARD RACE
FIRST SEASON	10.4	22.6	--
SECOND SEASON	10.2	21.8	52.6
THIRD SEASON	9.7	21.6	50.2
FOURTH SEASON	10.0	21.8	47.6

who kept on traveling down the road at full speed for another 100 yards. Amazingly, Eric was fine. He and his friend reconnected the sidecar with some rope, and they finished the trip, arriving safely at home.

Through all the ups and downs of his first two years in college, Eric endured. He continued to run. He remained in training. He had two more seasons ahead of him at the University of Edinburgh. But before the next season started, the course of his life would take a surprising turn.

5

A New Course

1923–1924

AT THE END OF MARCH 1923, a twenty-six-year-old man knocked on the door of 56 George Square in Edinburgh, the apartment where Eric lived with his brother Rob.

His name was David Patrick Thomson. He went by the initials DP, and some people who knew him jokingly said his initials stood for "Dynamic Personality"! That's because DP was excited about serving Jesus. And he was eager to ask Eric Liddell, the fast and famous runner, a question about serving Jesus.

In one week, DP would be traveling to Armadale, a small mining town in Scotland, 27 miles from Edinburgh. There, on Friday, April 6, 1923, he would try to gather a group of men so he could tell them about Jesus. People all over Scotland knew the name of Eric Liddell. So DP wanted to know if the twenty-one-year-old runner would come and speak at this meeting.

Eric was a strong Christian—regularly attending church services, helping others, and reading his Bible. But he had never before spoken in front of people. His brother Rob was eager to talk about Christianity, but Eric was shy, and a man of few words. He would feel like a fish out of water. Yet, just as with running, Eric knew God would help him to do the hard thing.

So when DP asked him to speak, Eric momentarily bowed his head in thought and prayer. He felt deep inside that he "was being called to do a piece of work."

Eric looked up and gave his answer: "All right, I'll come."

Eric had taken a brave step, and the Lord gave him encouragement. The next day a letter arrived all the way from China. Eric's sister, Jenny, had written weeks before and included this passage from Isaiah:

> Fear not, for I am with you;
> be not dismayed, for I am your God;
> I will strengthen you, I will help you,
> I will uphold you with my righteous right hand. (Isa. 41:10)

The promises of God and the timing of her letter helped give Eric strength.

At 9 p.m. the next Friday, Eric stood in front of about eighty men who had gathered in Armadale to hear "the Flying Scotsman." These were working men, their clothes coated with dust from the coal mine or brick factory. Eric told the men about his faith in Jesus Christ and how his faith related to his running. Afterward, Eric stayed and talked with many who had come. As DP Thomson later said, "Eric passed through what was perhaps the first great spiritual crisis of his life." It was the beginning of "a life of dedicated service that only death could end."

To Eric, this was a turning point. Now, in addition to running for God, he would also speak for him. And like his running style, his way of speaking was also unique. Although DP spoke with a big, deep voice, Eric's quiet Scottish accent and laid-back style made people feel like he was talking directly and personally with them. He didn't use fancy words but just spoke plainly about Jesus, sometimes "in scarcely more than a whisper."

Yet as he practiced, he also improved, and grew in confidence and ability, just as with running. After starting to speak about Jesus at public events, Eric himself began to notice change in himself. "Since then," Eric later recalled, "my awareness of being an active member of God's kingdom has been very real."

— What Did Eric Speak About? —

Here's a sample from one of Eric's public talks about Jesus. In this message, he talked about the word *sincere*, which he explained as coming from two Latin words, *sine* [without] and *cere* [wax].

> Some sculptors in ancient Rome used wax to disguise a chip on a statue. No one would see the flaw until the heat of the sun melted the wax or bad weather eroded it. In this way he wasn't being truly sincere. If we allow cracks and blemishes to appear in our faith, and then ignore them or attempt to cover them up, we aren't being truly sincere either. We must strive to make our faith the perfect work. We are then sincere to ourselves and sincere to God.

And DP saw the transformation: "You would hardly know he was the same man as six months ago. . . . I have never known a finer character in all my various experience. . . . He is pure gold, through and through."

Meanwhile, the pace of Eric's whole life was getting faster. All through his third season at the University of Edinburgh, in addition to running and taking classes, he now also continued to speak about Jesus. But all this busyness didn't slow Eric down. Instead, by June his running had caught fire! In every distance he ran, he was faster than he had been the year before.

July was his best month yet. During his first ever race in England—far warmer than the rainier weather of Scotland—Eric amazed spectators. At the Amateur Athletic Association Championship at Stamford Bridge, London, on July 6, he set a new British record for the 100-yards in a blazing 9.7 seconds! He never expected to do so well: "I surprised even myself!"

And one week later (as described in the first chapter of this book), he won the amazing come-from-behind victory at Stoke-on-Trent.

After his championship victory at Stamford Bridge, a Scottish newspaper, the *Glasgow Herald*, admired Eric's grit and determination, and said that Eric's

— Competing Against Eric —

How did Eric relate to the athletes he raced against? One unnamed athlete, a long-jumper, who competed at the 1923 Championship at Stamford Bridge watched Eric walk out onto the track. Here's what he saw:

> Eric had brought a small trowel [a hand-shovel] with him to dig his holes for starting . . . and he carefully went from one to another of his opponents in the race, and offered each the use of his trowel. Most of them (four, I seem to remember) accepted. All the nearby specta-

success was phenomenal. He "might even blossom into an Olympic hero."

But by April of 1924, as Eric started his fourth running season at Edinburgh, with the Paris Olympics only months away, many people didn't think of him as a hero. To them, Eric had become a traitor.

> tors appreciated the action (and a large number of athletes who recognized the Scottish champion had gathered to get as close a view as possible). All having prepared, he walked to each opponent again, and shook hands with him, smiling his very sunny smile.
>
> He then got "on his marks" with them, was off at the gun, and won a very fine race from the outside lane. I had heard a lot about him, and now I had seen him. I came away feeling that I had witnessed a gentleman doing all a gentleman should do. [Later], I realized that I had been watching a Christian in action.

6

Mounting Challenges

1924

SURPRISINGLY, the grass-surfaced running track at Craiglockhart Stadium in Edinburgh is not entirely flat. It's uneven. So that means that during his running career in Edinburgh, Eric actually ran many races uphill. But Eric trained for this—his practice runs included dashing up the steep and hilly streets of Edinburgh. And when you push yourself to sprint to the top—when you feel how hard it is, and you keep going—you're not just building speed. You're also gaining strength and endurance.

He would need it, because soon Eric would face another uphill battle.

In the Spring of 1924, Eric Liddell seemed to stand at the base of a huge mountain. At the top were the Olympic Games—just a few months away. But getting there would be hard.

About six months earlier, Eric had learned that the Olympic 100-meter race was scheduled to happen on a Sunday. The 100-meter was Eric's best race, but Sundays belonged to the Lord.

Eric believed that Sunday, like the Sabbath Day in the Old Testament, was supposed to be treated differently from the other six days of the week. Many Christians—then and now—honor this day of the week as a day of rest (the word "Sabbath" in the Bible means "to stop"). By doing this, these believers were trying to obey the fourth commandment ("Remember the Sabbath day, to keep it holy," Ex. 20:8). Some Christians thought that Jesus had fulfilled this Old Testament command and, therefore, it didn't apply to Christians. However, other Christians saw it as their duty to still obey this biblical command and make this day different ("holy") from the rest of the week. This was how Eric understood his responsibility to obey

— Going the Distance —

The standard race distances in Britain were measured in yards, while the standard Olympic race distances used the metric system of measurement (and still do).

British Race	Difference	Olympic Race
100 yards	is about 28 feet *shorter* than	100 meters
220 yards	is about 4 feet *longer* than	200 meters
440 yards	is about 8 feet *longer* than	400 meters

the fourth commandment. He believed Sundays were for church, rest, and serving the Lord.

So Eric asked the British Olympic Association about changing the date, but they didn't really try to help. After all, this had been the usual schedule for previous Olympics.

In those earlier Olympics, other athletes had felt the same way as Eric. In the 1908 Summer Olympics in London, one man had raced on a Sunday. Yet while posing for a photograph after the race, this runner insisted on holding a Bible in his hand! But Eric wouldn't take a half-way approach.

Earlier in his third season at Edinburgh, he had simply dropped out of a race that was on a Sunday. Instead, he had spoken at a church. He told the people there that each person had to be fully committed to the Lord, deciding whom to follow. Eric said, "Each one comes to the crossroads at some period of his life and must make his decision for or against his Master."

Eric wouldn't run on a Sunday, even if that meant he missed the 100-meter race at the Olympics. Some people thought Eric was doing the right thing. Others just thought he was odd or old-fashioned. But many thought he was ruining Britain's chances to win the gold medal! "A traitor to his country," people said. To some, the Flying Scotsman had now become the "most unpopular man in Britain."

But Eric knew what it was like to run uphill.

And he didn't quit. He embraced the pain. In addition to the 200-meter, Eric signed up for another race:

— Sundays During the Olympics —

When the first Sunday of the Paris Olympics arrived, instead of competing in the 100-meter race, Eric attended the Scots Presbyterian Church in Paris. (Sometimes this church is called the "Scots Kirk"; *kirk* is the Scottish word for "church.") On the second Sunday of the Olympics, Eric returned to the Scots Kirk. This time, he preached to a packed crowd. He spoke on Psalm 119:18 ("Open my eyes, that I may behold / wondrous things out of your law").

the quarter-mile (400 meters). This was a hard choice for Eric, a natural sprinter. Because the 400-meter requires so much strength and endurance, you couldn't sprint the entire race. People called it the "killer event."

Besides, people said that Eric was too short to do well at the 400 meters. Longer legs helped cover longer distances. Certainly it was true that the quarter-mile wasn't his best race. He had only run this distance a few times. And before the Olympics in July 1924, his best time was 50.2 seconds—slower than the Olympic record by a full two seconds.

And in the weeks before the Olympics, the climb seemed steeper than ever. When Eric ran in the Penn Relays, a famous track meet at the University of Pennsylvania in America, he did not do well at all. Besides getting seasick and losing his luggage on the voyage, he lost almost a week of exercise as he traveled back and forth across the Atlantic. But Eric saw hardship as preparation.

After arriving back in Scotland, Eric returned to training. His coach Tom McKerchar taught him a new strategy for running the 400 meters. For this distance, Eric said that he learned to run "the first hundred yards almost, if not quite, 'all out.' The back stretch at well over three-quarter pace. The next bend,

which one takes as the slowest part of the journey. The last hundred as a sprint."

And training on the track captured only part of Eric's attention. In the weeks before the Olympics, he was also studying for his final university exams. He was so busy, Eric admitted his running was not "absolutely at my top." (It probably didn't help that he had also hurt his leg in a friendly wrestling match with one of his roommates.)

But by the time Eric reached Paris for the Olympics, he had trained hard. He had faced steep hill after steep hill, and he had not given up. Still the question remained: Would he be ready?

7

Going for Gold

1924–1925

THE CEREMONIES FOR the 1924 Olympics opened on a blazing hot Saturday, July 5. Crowds swarmed into Colombe Stadium outside Paris, France. The concrete and steel stadium had been recently enlarged. Now 45,000 people could watch athletes compete on its 400-meter track and infield. For the opening ceremony, Eric and the other young men on his Olympic team joined athletes from around the world. Alongside their female teammates, they marched around the track wearing straw boater hats, white slacks, and navy blue suit coats with the British flag stitched onto the breast pocket.

The next day was Sunday, and Britain was not left without an athlete in the 100-meter race. Harold Abrahams, a friend and rival of Eric's, ran and won gold for Britain! Abrahams, alongside Americans Jackson Scholz and Charley Paddock, were also favored for the 200-meter. And in the 400-meter, others were ready to grab the gold. Two more Americans, Horatio Fitch and John Taylor, were top favorites! Did Eric even have a chance at a medal after skipping his best event to go to church?

Finally, on Tuesday, July 8, the day of Eric's first event arrived. He lined up to run the 200-meter race. Eric came in second in the quarter-finals, and the next day finished second in the semi-finals. Ninety minutes later, Eric raced in the finals. And he came in third, winning the bronze medal, with a time of 21.9 seconds.

The following day, July 10, Eric raced in the preliminary 400-meter heats. He finished his first round in 50.2 seconds and his second in 49.3 seconds. Yet he was not in the top three for either of these rounds. Most people didn't expect Eric Liddell to win anything, especially since the semi-finals and finals were the very next day. These grueling races would be the true test of his strength and endurance.

Yet for the semi-finals, he hit his best time yet for the 400-meter: a blazing 48.2 seconds. But the Olympic final was less than four hours away.

That wasn't much time to recover from such a fast race! And then he found out that for the finals, he was placed in the outside lane—not an ideal position. How would Eric do in his fourth quarter-mile race in thirty-six hours? One runner laughed Eric off as just "a sprinter," someone "who would pass out 50 yards from the finish."

His prediction came true in the final race—at least some of it. When the starter's pistol sounded, Eric exploded onto the track. Sprinting! With the full 400 meters still to go, Eric wasn't following Tom McKerchar's strategy at all. He was flying down the track *at full speed*! At the halfway mark, he was running so fast that his time was almost the gold-medal time—from the 200-meter event!

The other runners couldn't believe it. Surely, he had started too fast. No one could keep up this pace for the entire 400 meters! Any second, he would run out of energy and start to slow down.

"We went off to a perfect start," recalled Eric.

> But it was not until I got to the top of the straight that it suddenly dawned on me that I was several yards in front of the field. Evidently the pace I had set had been too much for the others up to this stage. The question was, could I last home? About seventy yards from the tape, I felt that the second man was at his nearest to me. I attempted to lengthen my stride and could do no more; but the comforting thought flashed into my

> mind that I could no longer hear the second man behind me. I was amazed to find that I had won by six yards.

The crowd exploded into cheers! 47.6 seconds. A new Olympic record! Tom McKerchar celebrated, but told Eric he must go lie down at the hotel and rest. But Eric had other plans: he was on his way to the telegraph station. He couldn't wait to send a message to his parents in China. He had won gold!

What did the other runners say about competing against Eric in the 400-meter Olympic final? American runner Horatio Fitch, the silver medal winner, later recalled how

> Liddell shot out of the block first, and he gained an early lead. He set a terrific pace down the first stretch, but I matched his speed. He was only two yards ahead. I heard the other runners behind us. I knew the duel would be between the two of us. Around the turn he held the same pace.

ERIC'S 1924 OLYMPIC RACE TIMES
(All times in seconds)

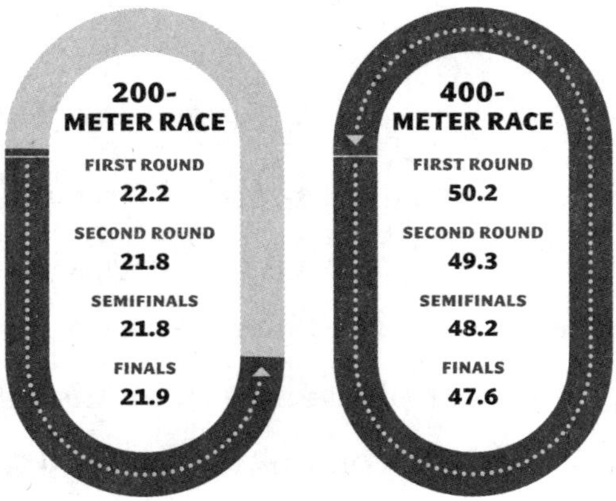

I couldn't believe a man could set such a pace and finish. . . . But Liddell pushed himself like a man possessed, head tilted back with determination. . . . I wasn't tired, but I couldn't go any faster. Every second I expected the Scot to slow down. . . . He had sprinted the entire race, an unusual feat because most coaches believed then that a runner could not sprint 400 yards. Liddell didn't weaken. And we were closing on the tape much too quickly. I pulled closer, but he strained until

> we were again the same distance apart. With the tape only 20 yards away, I again spurted closer, but Liddell threw his head further back, gathered himself together, and shot forward.

In the days after the race, Eric went back to Edinburgh—not a traitor but a hero!

After he graduated, his friends at Edinburgh University carried him around on their shoulders. Everyone loved Eric. And for the next year, wherever he traveled to speak, people flocked to see the Olympic champion.

Yet sometimes, Eric wanted to escape all the attention. Once when he was coming off a train in London, Eric noticed a waiting crowd of reporters. Always enjoying a joke, Eric also saw a porter, an employee in uniform who was helping with luggage. So Eric asked him if he could borrow his cap and luggage cart. So as newspaper men and reporters looked for the famous athlete, Eric slipped past unnoticed pretending to be a porter.

But most of the time, Eric was glad to talk to people. He didn't take the attention too seriously. When someone asked how he had won, Eric smiled and told them his secret strategy: "I run the first 200 meters as hard as I can. Then, for the second 200 meters, with God's help, I run harder."

But he was serious about other matters. On one occasion a reporter said, "One paper—*The Scotsman*—said you achieved immortality in Paris." Eric shook his head, "No sir. My immortality comes from Christ—not a track and field stadium in France."

For the next twelve months, Eric talked to men and women from all across England and Scotland and told them about Jesus Christ. He said, "We are placing before you during these few days the thing we have found to be best. We are setting before you one who is worthy of all our devotion—Christ. He is the Savior."

This year of traveling after the Olympics and talking about Jesus might have looked like a victory tour. But the busyness of that year introduced another difficulty for Eric. The challenge wasn't because the work was hard, but because the location wasn't right.

"I believe God made me for China," he would say. "And I am going to run a different race there."

— Running Hard —

For a year after his Olympic victory, Eric stayed extremely busy. Not only did he travel and speak all across England and Scotland, he also taught a Sunday school class at his church, and started taking a few seminary classes. (*Seminary* is a school where most of the students are preparing to become pastors or missionaries.) Although he wasn't planning to become a pastor, Eric studied what the Bible teaches (theology), how to study the Bible (hermeneutics), what Christians have done or taught in the past (church history), and how the Bible relates to daily life (practical application).

8

A Different Race

1925–1931

IN JULY 1924 newspaper headlines across England had proclaimed Eric Liddell's gold medal victory. That same year his father had written a very different report—not about events in Paris, but about the situation for foreigners living in China.

"The feeling all round is one of suspense," he

wrote, "not knowing what will happen next." Seven years before, China had decided to support England in World War I. So China and Great Britain signed a treaty. As allies, they promised they would help each other if attacked. But when World War I was over, Great Britain did not keep its promise. Instead, they allowed Japan to have some parts of China.

This made people all across China angry and suspicious of anyone from Great Britain. And before long, if you were a foreigner living in China, you were often in danger of being attacked by unruly mobs. Even missionaries had been kidnapped and killed. So by the time Eric was on his way to China, his father could say that "the waters are boiling."

Yet in July of 1925, Eric, now twenty-three years old, was traveling east by train for China. For two grueling weeks, the railcars crossed Europe and Russia, including over 5,000 miles on the Trans-Siberian Railway. When he finally arrived in China, he spent part of August vacationing at the beach in Peitaiho with his family (his parents, his older brother Rob and his wife, his younger brother Ernest, and his sister, Jenny). His parents still served as missionaries. Rob was now a medical doctor in Siaochang, while Jenny and Ernest still lived at home.

He hadn't seen his entire family for three years, and together they enjoyed the ocean and wooden beach houses they had loved when Eric was a child. Over the next three weeks, sometimes they'd sit under the veranda, talking or reading, shaded from the blazing 110-degree August heat. At other times, they'd swim in the cold shallow green water or walk along wide shores of fine yellow sand.

After their vacation was over, everyone except Rob went back to Tientsin. This is where his family served the London Missionary Society, and where Eric would start teaching students at the Anglo-Chinese college.

Back in 1902, an Englishman named Samuel Lavington Hart had started this school (elementary through high school) with fifty students. Dr. Hart had left his life in England because he wanted to offer an excellent Christian education to the children of Chinese leaders. He had a goal: to shape the next generation in China for Christ.

The boarding school was surrounded by an eight-foot wall and located within a special section of Tientsin reserved for foreigners. So it was isolated from most of the horrible conditions that were devastating China. Outside of cities like Tientsin, problems like disease, illiteracy, cruelty, violence, and poverty were common. Many people lived in shacks and worked long hours in fields of wheat, millet, peanuts, or rice. Farmers labored to protect their crops from drought, floods, heat, cold, and ravaging hordes of locusts.

Eric knew about these problems. He knew that he couldn't fix them all. But he could do something. At the University of Edinburgh, he had run and studied science, and now, at the Anglo-Chinese college, for about five hundred boys, ages eight to eighteen, he would teach them sports and science.

Eric loved being a teacher, and it didn't take long for students to love his teaching. He quickly became a favorite teacher. Eric both lectured in the classroom and also set up experiments in the laboratory. One time, Eric mixed together several chemicals, creating a terrible-tasting but harmless liquid. Eric told the class that it was delicious. To prove it, he acted like he had tasted it: he dipped his index finger into the awful substance, and then licked his second finger.

— Learning for Life —

What was Eric like as a teacher? David McGavin, one of Eric's colleagues at the Anglo-Chinese college, remembered Eric's ministry among the boys of the school. Just like in Eric's world-class running, David said, "In his teaching at the college, Eric maintained the same high standard. And his influence among the boys was very great. His Bible classes, taught outside of school hours, were very well attended. I remember the joy with which he would tell us of boys who had committed their lives to Christ."

Of course, as soon as his students tried it for themselves, they realized their teacher had played a joke on them.

Eric taught the boys how to play rugby and tennis—and, of course, how to run. He also coached the school's soccer team (though they called it "football"). And just like in teaching, Eric had fun in athletics as well. Sometimes he would play tennis—against *himself*. He would hit the ball gently across the net, then race to the other side of the court and hit it back. He also let his students run a 100-meter race against him. On a six-lane track, Eric would give his students a 10-meter head start to make it a bit fairer. Sometimes he won, and sometimes his students beat him. Eric didn't mind. He loved his students and was glad when they did well.

Although Eric decided that he would not compete in the 1928 Olympics in Amsterdam in the Netherlands, he still loved to run. In 1930, he ran in his last competitive race in the North China Championship. At twenty-eight years old, he participated in the 100-meter and 400-meter races, and won both! But when a reporter asked him if he missed running, Eric admitted, "Of course, it's natural for a chap to think over all that sometimes, but I'm glad I'm in the work I'm engaged in now. A fellow's life counts for far more at this than the other. Not a corruptible

— Teaching Teenagers —

Reflecting on his ministry as a teacher, Eric wrote:

> The Spirit of our Master slowly works his way into our games, work, and services. Just like a builder does, we do not see great changes in a week or two. Instead, here and there comes a word of cheer and a sight that makes you sure that the work is slow but sure. For example, in one situation, a boy begins to face life and definitely decides that he will face it building his life with Christ as its foundation, and in another situation, a different boy quietly makes his surrender to Christ too.

crown, but an incorruptible, you know?" Eric knew how to answer because he knew his Bible. He was thinking about 1 Corinthians 9:24–27:

> Do you not know that in a race all the runners run, but only one receives the prize? So run that you may obtain it. Every athlete exercises self-control in all things. They do it to receive a perishable wreath, but we an imperishable. So I do not run aimlessly; I do not box as one beating the air. But I discipline my body and keep it under control, lest after preaching to others I myself should be disqualified.

Eric also loved to run the race and follow Jesus in other areas of his life. During the week he helped lead the school's morning chapel service and organized an after-school Bible study at his house. And on Sundays at the nearby English-speaking church, Eric taught Sunday school and sometimes preached.

During his twelve years of teaching at the college, Eric taught hundreds of students. And over 160 of them became Christians. Eric wanted all his students to learn and mature, to grow and change. Yet before those dozen years were over, the teacher himself would learn and grow.

China's biggest problems weren't in the cities, like Tientsin. The real suffering and the real needs were

in the countryside. Eric wanted to help; he wanted to do more. And by 1931, he was starting to consider a wider field in which to labor, other lanes in which to run.

9

Changing Lanes

1931–1937

DURING THE YEARS THAT ERIC taught at the Anglo-Chinese college, violence grew and raged across China. Back in 1927, conflict had erupted into a civil war. Now, four years later, over eight thousand soldiers protected the city of Tientsin where Eric taught, but the surrounding countryside was dangerous. On a trip outside Tientsin, a friend of Eric's, who also taught at the college, was robbed and shot to death. In 1929, five missionaries had been killed and others were hurt. The next year, ninety-seven missionaries had been kidnapped and thirty-three killed.

Then things got worse. In September 1931, Japan invaded China. The Japanese government saw an opportunity—if China was fighting itself in a civil war, that meant they were weak and more easily taken over. Now there were three armies fighting all across China: two Chinese armies (Nationalists and Communists) and the Japanese army. And wherever there was fighting, there was suffering. Soldiers killed soldiers and civilians. Villages were destroyed, homes were robbed, and crops were ruined.

Eric wanted to help people. But if in the future Eric was going to work in the countryside, he knew it wouldn't be in schools. Outside the cities, Eric would need to be serving in churches, and that meant he would need to become a pastor. So when

Eric went back to Scotland in the summer of 1931, it wasn't for rest and vacation.

For twelve months Eric lived in Scotland and, going to seminary at the Scottish Congregational college in Glasgow, he trained to become a pastor. He had studied the Bible before; now he was going in deeper. He dove deep into theology (what the Bible teaches), and also into Hebrew and Greek (the ancient languages that the Bible had first been written in).

Yet Eric was not just growing in knowledge. God was also growing his heart. Through helpful conversations with friends, Eric grew to have even deeper trust in what Jesus had done for him. He also grew in greater obedience to what Jesus expected from him. As he later explained in his book *The Disciplines of the Christian Life*, this meant, "absolute honesty, absolute purity, absolute unselfishness, absolute love." He had learned these four somewhat famous principles from DP Thomson, yet over time, he had made them his own. And the Lord had started to change him. Deep within, Eric said, began to grow a "greater willingness to share the deepest things in my own life."

While in Scotland, he was ordained (officially recognized as a pastor) by the Scottish Congregational Church, and he also became connected with the London Missionary Society. And in all his spare time, Eric traveled across England and Scotland, preaching in churches and meeting with people. Crowds gathered to hear this legendary runner who had gone to distant China.

Eric invited them to serve in missions too. But, he told them, they didn't need to travel far from home to serve Christ. They were already on mission, right where they lived. "We are all missionaries. We carry our religion with us, or we allow our religion to carry us. Wherever we go, we either bring people nearer to Christ, or we repel them from Christ."

When his year in Great Britain was over, Eric boarded a ship to return to China. As he stood on the deck, he could recall the names of many men and women who had devoted their lives to missions. Yet one stood out above all the rest.

Eric Liddell had met Florence MacKenzie at a church service in 1926. Her parents had grown up in Canada, but were now missionaries to China. Florence loved playing the organ and wanted to one day serve in missions as a nurse.

Three years later, in 1929, Eric and Florence (Eric often called her "Flossy") had begun dating. And after a year of dating in 1930, he had asked her to marry him, and she had said, "Yes." But the next few years wouldn't be easy for the engaged couple. Before long, Eric would sail to Scotland for seminary, yet he and Florence kept in touch, writing letters or telegrams, even while he was far away.

So two years after he had returned from Scotland as an ordained pastor, Eric Henry Liddell and Florence Jean MacKenzie were married on March 27, 1934, in the Union Church in Tientsin, China. Photographs of the young couple showed that Eric and Florence loved each other and loved to have fun. In one photo, their faces beamed with smiles as they walked, just married, out of the church. In another, they were cracking up, as Eric grabbed Florence's hat and wore it upside down on his own head. And in another candid shot, they both laughed as

— The Real Eric —

As Florence dated Eric, she had seen that the famous athlete was truly a kind and godly man. Here's how she described him. Florence learned that Eric's daily time in the Bible was "the mainspring of his life." He was "strict on himself," but a "peacemaker" with others. "It used to stagger me," recalled Florence, "the way people would disagree violently with him and say the bitterest things. He would smile and pass it off. He was incredibly forgiving and thought nothing was accomplished by losing one's temper. He was so understanding of other people. He always seemed to be able to put himself in the shoes of somebody else."

Florence tried to escape Eric's attempts to tickle her ribs.

Together, Eric and Florence loved each other, and they loved the people of China. For the next two years, they lived in Tientsin. They settled into married life, and for now Eric resumed teaching and loving his students at the Anglo-Chinese college.

The following year, Eric and Florence had a daughter: Patricia (b. July 1935). If Eric ventured into the countryside during this season, he wouldn't take his young family with him. It was far too dangerous. Local warlords fought Chinese soldiers for control of thousands of tiny villages throughout China. This fighting had destroyed lives and families and homes and crops. So many places needed help, including the town of Siaochang, where Eric had grown up.

Yet more and more, Eric thought about going into the countryside to help people and share the gospel. He was ordained now and ready to go, and missionaries were desperately needed. Yet Eric didn't feel that the timing was right for him to move into the countryside.

Then in 1936, the London Missionary Society asked Eric if he would quit teaching in Tientsin and move to Siaochang. But Eric still did not think that God had called him to go. Not yet. At this point, Florence was pregnant with their second baby, who was born in January 1937. They named her Heather. Eric continued to feel God's call to serve his students at the college.

Yet over the next year, while Eric taught and discipled students in Tientsin, the situation began to change. During this time, the Chinese government wanted everyone to prepare for the next wave of anticipated Japanese attacks. So students at the college were forced to start wearing military uniforms. War was coming.

And the next year, that's exactly what happened. In July 1937, Japan once again sent an army into the country of China. A few months later, even the city of Tientsin fell under Japanese control. Although the city was still safer than the countryside, life was now different. Eventually, over the next eight years, the number of major battles waged on Chinese soil rose to more than a thousand, and the number of people killed to more than 15 million. Suffering and sickness and starvation filled the countryside.

Eric loved his family, and he didn't want to leave them. Yet he also loved the people of China who were suffering. How could he help most? "What exactly do we have that we can give?" he would ask himself. His answer? "What we have to give the Chinese is the love of God in their hearts."

So in late 1937 Eric told the London Missionary Society that the timing was now right. He would go to Siaochang. But his family would stay behind in Tientsin, where it was safer.

In December 1937, Eric and his older brother, Rob, began a 400-mile trek. Over the next ten days, they sailed on barges, rode on trains, and were twice robbed at gunpoint. When they finally reached their destination, the town where they had grown up, Eric looked at his brother and said, "So this is Siaochang." The next phase of his missionary life had begun.

10

Running Risks

1937–1943

THOUSANDS OF TINY VILLAGES dotted the massive countryside around Siaochang. All across the Great Plains, Chinese and Japanese soldiers constantly fought to take or retake control of villages. "Over such an extended territory," Eric wrote, "there could be up to 100 fights like this every single day."

Over the next eighteen months, Eric met with people all across the area. He rode his bike down countless dirt paths damaged by war. He wore a Red Cross armband, to show that he was peaceful, not a soldier. But many men and women already knew who he was. They remembered his father and how he had served them years ago. In time, the people around Siaochang came to call Eric "Pastor Liddell" (*Li Mu Shi*), the same name they had called his father.

When visiting a village, Eric tried to meet the needs he faced that day. Depending on what he discovered, he would meet with families in their homes, he would encourage Christians, he would lead a church service, or he would organize an evangelistic meeting. And everywhere he went in this war-torn land, Eric tried to spread peace.

Through his words, Eric wanted others to know the ultimate peace—being right with God through Jesus Christ. And through his example, Eric lived out the peace of God. In this war, he didn't choose to help only one side. Eric helped villagers, Chinese National soldiers, Chinese Communist soldiers, and Japanese soldiers—everyone. Despite the risks and the warfare, Eric saw God at work: "Through the grace of God, we have been able to carry on our work in China."

When he was in Siaochang, Eric sometimes helped his brother Rob as he did medical work at the hospital. Another missionary, Annie Buchan

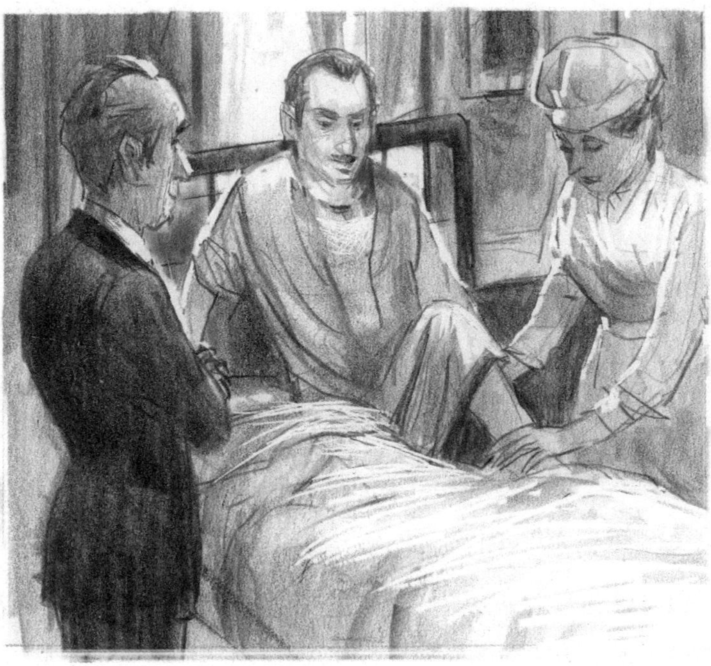

from Scotland, was a nurse in Siaochang and a friend of the Liddell brothers. Years later, she recalled how Eric served in those days of war:

> Eric's methods—in steadily visiting the churches, preparing plans, drawing maps, and holding regular conferences with the Chinese preachers—were never complicated, but simple, clear, and direct, just like his own character. In Siaochang our preachers, nurses, and students hung on his words, and "the common people heard him gladly." He was an extraordinarily fearless person; he had this awareness of Jesus being with him all the time.

All the fighting made it difficult to travel and to get news from home. But Eric was able to make the dangerous 400-mile journey back to Tientsin a few times. He loved being with his family. When they were apart, he missed them with all his heart. Yet through this hard time, the Lord was faithful.

One time Annie asked Eric if ever he regretted coming to Siaochang. Immediately Eric answered: "Never."

Eric told her how the Lord was sustaining him and helping him face even the ever-changing challenges of Siaochang. "I have more joy and freedom in the work than I have ever experienced before," he said.

But the risks in Siaochang were getting worse. Japanese soldiers now seemed to be everywhere. People were being shot or kidnapped. As winter set in, everyone faced the threat of starvation, sickness, and even frostbite. Families took shelter wherever they could, even in burned-out houses. And still Eric got on his bike and went out to serve.

Then, in 1939, even as World War II was breaking out around the globe, Eric and his family were once again able to go home to Scotland together. During their time away, they saw friends and family. Jenny had been married for seven years and was living with her husband in Carcant, Scotland, 80 miles south of Drymen where Eric's parents had retired. Yet sadly,

Eric's father had passed away before they arrived, and Eric's old running coach, Tom McKerchar, would die right as they were leaving to return to China. Eric grieved these losses, yet not without hope. And through the days ahead, he found that keeping himself busy was "the best thing possible for me."

On their return voyage, from Scotland to China, although their boat sailed as part of a fleet of ships for protection, German forces attacked their convoy. Ships around them were torpedoed and sunk. "We were running for our lives," Florence later said. But God spared their ship, and by the end of 1940, the Liddells were back in China: Florence and the girls were in Tientsin, and Eric was back in Siaochang.

By now there were over a million Japanese soldiers in China. And the fighting and the destruction were worse than ever. Japanese soldiers forced people to repair roads and construct walls as if they were slaves. Eric continued to ride his bike wherever he could help. Once on a way to a wedding, he was mistaken for an enemy soldier and shot at—twice! (Thankfully, they must not have had very good aim.) And then when the hospital where his brother worked needed more staff, Eric agreed to be the new superintendent. Even though he was not a doctor, he could try to keep the hospital running smoothly.

And then, five months later, the Japanese authorities made another announcement: all the foreigners had to leave Siaochang. So Eric went back to

— Song for the Soul —

While Eric traveled and ministered around Siaochang, he taught the Chinese Christians a song: "Be Still, My Soul." Eric taught this hymn in whatever language people spoke: English or Mandarin. (There are two main Chinese dialects—Mandarin covers the majority of the country, while Cantonese is spoken in some southern regions.)

Eric wanted these Chinese believers to be reminded that no matter what happened to them, the Lord was their friend, their guide, and the ruler of all. Here are the lyrics to the first verse of "Be Still, My Soul" in English and Mandarin.

***Be Still, My Soul* 我靈鎮靜**

Be still, my soul, the Lord is on your side
我靈鎮靜　主正在你身旁
Bear patiently the cross of grief or pain
憂傷十架　務要忍耐擔當
Leave to your God to order and provide
信靠父神　由祂安排主張
In every change, God faithful will remain
萬變之中　惟主信實久長
Be still, my soul, your best, your heavenly
    friend
我靈鎮靜　天友最是善良
Through thorny ways leads to a joyful end
經過荊棘　引到歡樂之疆

* Kathrina von Schlegel, "Be Still, My Soul," trans. Jane Borthwick (1752; 1855). The Chinese text is from "Be Still, My Soul," *Christian Psalms of Praise (English and Chinese)* (blog), July 26, 2021, https://chinasundayschool.wordpress.com.

Florence and their daughters in Tientsin. But even life in the city of Tientsin had become dangerous. Eric had a decision to make: How could he keep his family safe? Within weeks, Eric sent his family to safety in Canada to be near Florence's family. There their third daughter, Maureen, was born in September 1941. Eric received the news through a telegram, and he immediately replied with his own short message: "Wonderful news!"

Yet for now all he could do was write. The London Missionary Society wanted Eric to stay in China. The Society had released Rob from his medical missionary duty and allowed him to return to his family in Scotland. But the missionary society had other hopes for Eric. He was to continue his missionary work in China—preaching and teaching—until "conditions render this impossible."

But for Eric, serving in Tientsin already seemed nearly impossible. All foreigners were placed under travel restrictions. They couldn't leave the city, and news from the outside world hardly ever reached them. Christians were forbidden to meet as churches. So Eric tried to adjust his approach again, and for the next fourteen months, he met with small groups of Christians for "tea church." If it was less than ten people who gathered "for tea," these services would not attract attention of the Japanese authorities.

During this time, Eric stayed in Tientsin with the family of Pastor Howard Smith. And wherever he could, Eric served them too. He played with their children, teaching them tennis, cricket, and how to play a card game called Bridge. He helped the children start a stamp collection, and he did chores for the family around the house. Every morning, he left the house at 5 a.m. to buy bread for the family from a local bakery. And once, after a nighttime dust storm, he got up even earlier to clean the entire house before the family was awake. Eric was glad to serve and give whatever kind of help was needed.

Years later Pastor Smith remembered how "I never saw Eric angry. I never heard him say a cross or unkind word. He just 'went about doing good.' . . . The pattern of his daily living had so few faults because he offered up, quite simply, each smallest thing to Christ."

And Eric's living like Christ was sustained by his learning about Christ. Since Eric was unable to leave the city, he had more time to deeply study the life and teachings of Jesus. And what he was learning, he wanted others to know too. So he wrote a book: *The Disciplines of the Christian Life*. In it, Eric said, "The Christian life should be a life of growth. I believe the secret of growth is to develop the devotional life," practicing godly habits like daily prayer and Bible reading.

And then on March 12, 1943, the Japanese authorities made yet another announcement. All British and American citizens, the "enemies" of the Axis Powers (Germany, Italy, and Japan), had to move to a special camp in Shantung Province, 400 miles southeast of Tientsin.

After packing his two suitcases and saying his goodbyes to the Howard Smith family and Chinese friends, Eric boarded the train to his new home: the Weihsien Internment Camp. His new place to serve.

11

To the Breaking Point

1943–1944

FOR THE NEXT 694 DAYS, Eric's new home was a prison camp. Weihsien meant "Courtyard of the Happy Way." But during World War II, this camp was not known for its happiness.

The Weihsien property had originally been built as a missionary center for American Presbyterians. Yet by the time Eric entered in March 1943, the buildings and grounds had seen years of decay and destruction from war and bandits. None of the toilets worked (there was no running water), so prisoners used holes in the ground that then had to regularly be emptied with buckets and carried outside the camp. There was no heating or air conditioning, so winter temperatures plunged below freezing and summer heat

— Eric's New Home —

Eight-foot walls surrounded the Weihsien prison camp—electrified barbed wire hummed along the top, and soldiers with machine guns stood watch in towers at each corner. A few open areas within the camp contained trees or gardens. But most of the space was crammed with dozens of brick buildings—camp headquarters, a camp store, a three-story hospital, a school, kitchen, dining hall, assembly hall, and lots of barracks where prisoners lived, some for men and some for women.

soared near 100° F. Everyone was dirty, with most prisoners only being allowed one shower a week, using water carried by hand.

Everyone was crowded. Over 1,800 men, women, and children lived crammed into a space slightly larger than three soccer fields. Eric shared a room that was 9-feet wide and 12-feet long with two other missionary men, and later a fourth man was crammed into their small space. In that tiny area, Eric kept the small number of items he had brought with him: a few clothes, eating utensils, photographs of his family, a Bible, some books (including *The Pilgrim's Progress*), curtains to use as bedsheets, a few medals from running, two watches (one was his and the other had been his father's), and one pair of dark gray spiked running shoes.

Everyone was also hungry. While there was plenty of bread and often vegetables, most people lost weight from the poor diet. Breakfast was only two pieces of bread and some porridge. Lunch was a lumpy gray stew made from eggplant. And dinner featured leftovers from lunch, which the prisoners called "S.O.S." (same old stew). Within a year or so, Eric had secretly made arrangements to sell his medals to someone who lived outside the camp so he could buy more food for those on the inside.

Then there were animals. Bugs were everywhere—flies, mosquitos, and red-brown bedbugs that infested mattresses and left bloody bite marks. And there were so many rats that prisoners started a competition to kill off the disease-infested rodents. One three-man team killed sixty-eight rats in a single day. Yet no matter how many rats were killed, dozens more would appear.

These awful conditions characterized life inside Weihsien, and so did the regular schedule. Each day began abruptly—a horn blared to wake everyone at 7:15 a.m. Prisoners had fifteen minutes to be ready for roll call, when soldiers would count the prisoners to make sure no one was missing. The prisoners in this camp came from all nations and backgrounds. There were missionaries (over two hundred of them), musicians, carpenters, nurses, teachers, and almost one hundred children without their parents. And throughout the camp, you could hear all sorts of languages, with prisoners coming from eleven different countries, including England, Scotland, Iran, Cuba, Panama, Russia, India, Italy, Belgium, and Holland.

After getting up and being counted, each prisoner had a job. Some worked in the hospital, kitchens, or gardens, and some emptied the toilets. Others washed or mended clothing by hand, or pumped and carried fresh water from a well. Thirty armed guards also lived in the camp, but as long as prisoners did their work, the guards basically left them alone.

Sometimes, these terrible conditions made people grumpy or angry, and occasional fights would break out.

Even though he was suffering along with everyone else, Eric tried to be cheerful. One prisoner said that Eric had an "unruffled spirit" and "constantly smiling face." Another said, "He never let anyone see him downcast."

And he also tried to help other people in whatever ways he could. A fellow-prisoner remembered that Eric "threw himself into it to make others feel better about the situation all of us were in." God gave Eric strength to endure and to serve, and Eric served to glorify God.

How could Eric set such an example? Each morning, long before roll call, Eric would light a small

lamp and read his Bible and pray. Every day he prayed for his family and fellow prisoners. And, in time, for his enemies. "I've begun to pray for the guards," he said. "And it's changed my whole attitude toward them." Eric's time with God each morning was, he said, like cleansing "the dust" from his eyes, preparing him to face the day. And Eric needed the Lord's daily strength.

In addition to his own job—teaching the imprisoned children math and science—Eric did more. Lots more. He organized church services and taught a Bible class for anyone inside Weihsien. And on top of teaching, he helped other people with their jobs. He helped in the kitchen and assisted with laundry. He cleaned toilets, chopped wood, pumped water, swept floors, carried supplies, moved furniture, and carted away the garbage. "I once saw him unloading supplies from the back of a cart," recalled one prisoner. "I said to myself: Why is he doing it? That's someone else's responsibility. Later I realized he did everything. It was said he was worth ten men. I can believe it."

Additionally, Eric created opportunities for the children and teens to have fun—to play chess, square dance, make model boats, and put on a puppet show. He also organized athletic competitions

— Strength for Today —

A. P. Cullen, who had taught Eric at Eltham College, later became a fellow missionary in China. Here's how someone who'd known Eric for most of his life described him:

> Let no one think that Eric didn't have his temptations, just as we have: temptations to laziness, carelessness, compromise, and what not. But Eric won his way through, by persistent study, regular times of devotion, constantly meditating on God's word, diligently praying, getting up early in the morning and spending one hour—two hours—in a concentrated search for God's will as revealed in the teaching of Jesus and the Bible generally.

in basketball, hockey, soccer, baseball, softball, and running.

In the summer of 1943, Eric put on his spiked running shoes to compete in a camp race. In order to create a 220-yard course, the track looped around the camp four times. As the runners took their marks, Eric gave the others a head start. But although weakened by prison life, Eric still knew how to run—and how to win. On the final lap, Eric pulled ahead of the other runners, threw his head back, and beat them all by a huge gap. Everyone loved seeing this famous athlete run once again.

They were also grateful to speak with him. Eric would take time to encourage people who were struggling with being lonely, depressed, angry, or afraid. He took long walks around Weihsien, having quiet conversations with men and women who needed encouragement and prayer. And Eric also spent time listening and supporting the kids and teens, who had started calling him "Uncle Eric." And to let his young friends know if he was available to talk, Eric started hanging a sign at the entrance to his room, "Eric Is In" or "Eric Is Out."

Many people in the camp also struggled with physical sicknesses like malaria and scarlet fever. Others felt the effects of not enough food, not enough water, and not enough sleep. So did Eric.

A year after that first 220-yard camp race, Eric organized another Sports Day for all the prisoners. Once again, he prepared to run, but this time, people noticed a difference. He looked sick and slightly stooped. And thinner—his weight had dropped from 160 pounds to 130.

When the race began, Eric was at the front, but on the last lap, he couldn't keep up. And another man, twenty-four-year-old Aubrey Grandon, surged ahead of Eric to win the race. When the competition was over, Eric joyfully rushed to congratulate the winner.

In days ahead, Eric continued to work and serve. But something was different now. Something was wrong.

12

The Final Lap

1944–1945

IN JULY 1944, Eric's friend Annie Buchan was forced to move to the Wiehsien prison camp. When she arrived, she couldn't believe her eyes. She knew Eric well from serving together at the hospital in Siaochang just a few years before. But something had happened to Eric that her trained nurse's eye couldn't ignore. His eyes were sunken, his legs were scrawny, and his skin looked gray. His movements were slower, and so was his speech. Something wasn't right, yet he continued to serve others.

Then prison life became harder. That summer was especially hot, and the following winter especially cold. And when a new commander came to run the camp, some prisoners tried to escape. As punishment, the new commander gave all the prisoners even less food than normal. Some people began to fight over food because they were so hungry. The guards grew edgy. Still Eric continued to serve.

Yet he began to have regular headaches and food started to smell awful to him. He would feel dizzy and lose his balance. As Eric tried to work, sometimes he was just too weak.

Then in January of 1945, Eric caught the flu, and he could hardly walk. Yet he dragged himself out of bed to preach the following Sunday. Then on February 11, 1945, Eric suffered a stroke. A stroke damages the brain because the blood supply is interrupted. With these symptoms, Annie wondered if he might have a brain tumor.

He wasn't his normal self. She remembered that one day he told her the future seemed clouded in shadows. He said that "everything seemed black. This wasn't like him," Annie recalled. "He'd always been full of hope." That winter, when a fellow prisoner needed shoes in that freezing weather, Eric gave away his running shoes.

A few weeks later, Eric thought he felt a bit better. As he had done so many times before, Eric wrote an encouraging letter to his wife and daughters. Later he was seen walking around the camp for fifteen minutes, listening and giving advice to another prisoner. The person who saw him recalled that "as usual, he was smiling."

On Wednesday, February 21, 1945, Eric led his usual Bible study. The topic was surrender to God's will. His speech was slow, and he needed to lie down as he talked. Suddenly, in the middle of the discussion, Eric's body went rigid and tight. He was having another stroke.

Annie rushed to help her friend. He was immediately taken to the camp hospital, where he had another stroke that same evening. Then at 9:20 p.m., Eric Liddell died.

Everyone was shocked. This Olympic athlete—who seemed super-human in strength, who had cheerfully served and given life to others—had been taken in death.

Eric had known he was sick and getting weaker. He knew that God had a plan for his life, and that God knew how long his life would last. He knew that his life—his running and his serving—was submitted to God and for God's glory. His final words capture what he believed: "It is surrender."

At Eric's funeral service, the camp gathered to mourn and to remember Eric Henry Liddell. People shared comments and prayers, and they all sang one of Eric's favorite hymns, "Be Still, My Soul." When

the service was over, three days after his death, Eric was buried in a small graveyard within the prison.

But it would take three months for Florence to hear about her husband's death. Two friends from church came to her house and shared the news. The Red Cross had been notified and passed along the sad news to Florence's church. Yet it took five more months until she learned that he had died of a brain tumor. With the limited medical resources at Weihsien, there was nothing anyone could have done to have cured his condition. Florence tried to comfort her three daughters now grieving again. For Eric's 73-year-old mother had passed away just ten months before, and now their dear father was gone at the age of forty-three.

For months, tears were a familiar sight in the Liddell household. And for the rest of their lives, Florence, Patricia, Heather, and Maureen deeply grieved the tragic loss of their husband and father.

Yet God comforted and helped Eric's family. At times, one daughter struggled with anger at losing a father she hardly remembered. Another of his daughters later admitted that the grieving took time: "Slowly I began to appreciate how much he had meant to others—and how much others relied on him. That was his purpose. He belonged to everyone else in the world as well as to us. I understood we were meant to share him."

The world grieved Eric's death as well. All over the globe, thousands of people attended memorial services for Eric—in Toronto, Canada, and in Edinburgh and Glasgow, Scotland.

Florence lived for almost forty more years, until her death in 1984. Eric's brother Rob lived until 1973, and his brother Ernest until 1975, while his sister Jenny lived until 1994.

Yet Eric's legacy would live on. Through books and even movies (including *Chariots of Fire* and *On Wings of Eagles*), he was remembered as an Olympic athlete, a record-holding, medal-winning runner. But the people who knew him best remembered more than an athlete. To them, Eric Liddell was also a

Christian and missionary who ran the race of life—not for personal fame, but to display the excellence of his Savior.

That's how Eric wanted others to think of him. During his life, thousands came to hear his words and hundreds wrote articles about him and his

— Remembering Eric Liddell —

David McGavin, a colleague who also served in China, wrote:

> It is said that to really know a person you have to live in the same house with them. I had this privilege—to share an apartment with Eric and two of his colleagues in Tientsin, and I found that, at home, as elsewhere, Eric's life glorified God. Eric Liddell was the most Christlike man I ever knew.

Harold Abrahams, a fellow Olympic athlete at the Paris games, wrote:

accomplishments. To them, Eric said, "When you speak of me, give the glory to my master, Jesus Christ."

And that's how Eric viewed his own life. Running was never ultimate or even terribly important. "I never prayed that I would win a race," he had

> Eric Liddell was a man whose intense spiritual convictions contributed largely to his athletic triumphs. While his ability must have been great, if it were not for the profound intensity of his spirit, he surely could not have achieved so much.

His friend DP Thomson wrote:

> His was the most consistent Christian character, as well as one of the most attractive and winning of personalities of any man I have ever known closely. With it all went his unfailing sense of humor—"that smiling face, with the twinkling blue eyes."

said. To Eric, even Olympic achievement was for a higher goal: "I have, of course, prayed about the athletic meetings, asking that in this, too, God might be glorified."

There is no grave stone for Eric Liddell. When he was buried in Weihsien, only a wooden cross marked his grave. Today that cross is long gone.

Instead, a statue and a memorial stand at the site of the prison camp in Weihsien, now called Weifang. The statue, made of bronze, shows a life-sized Eric in his Olympic days, running with head thrown back and straining toward a finish line.

Beside the statue stands a 7-foot memorial, a slab of Scottish granite, 2-feet wide. Chiseled into its brown surface flecked with black and gray, almost one hundred English words stand out in gold lettering. The lines summarize the life and strength and impact of Eric Henry Liddell.

And then four lines in Mandarin—lines from the last half of Isaiah 40:31—point toward the source of Eric's power to never give up.

他們應可振翅高飛
如展翼的雄鷹
他們應可競跑向前
永遠不言疲累

They shall mount up with wings like eagles;
they shall run and not be weary;
they shall walk and not faint. (Isa. 40:31b)

Conclusion

Lessons from a Life

ERIC LIDDELL WAS A CHRISTIAN, a husband and father, an Olympic athlete, and a missionary.

He truly seemed to excel at whatever he did. He tried to faithfully follow Jesus, and he deeply loved his family. He sacrificially served others, and he was one of the fastest runners of his day.

People recognized his accomplishments. He raced

before thousands. He won medals and prizes and trophies. He wrote a book and traveled across the globe. And he received invitations to speak to huge crowds. Most of his life, Eric was famous.

But Eric didn't race or write or teach or travel because he wanted people to like him or to say nice things about him. He didn't care about being famous or popular. Instead, he aimed to shine a spotlight on someone else.

Eric Liddell lived for the glory of God. But what does that mean?

When you win a gold medal or set a world record, that means you're the best in that sporting event. In his day, no one was better than Eric Liddell in the 100-, 200-, or 400-meter races. He was fast! That's what made him a unique and special athlete. Just like the glory of a giraffe is its height, or the glory of the Nile River is its length, the glory of some thing or person is what sets it apart from everything else.

And God is glorious for being God (Isa. 42:8; 48:11). There's no one like him! The Bible teaches that God is perfect in every way (Ps. 18:30). He's perfectly loving, perfectly faithful, perfectly holy, perfectly patient, and perfectly good. No one is more loving or faithful or holy or patient or good than God is (2 Sam. 7:22; Jer. 10:6)!

That's his glory! He is God. He's the only one and in a class by himself!

For when you see what God is like—in all his incredible glory—it's stunning! Brilliant! Magnificent! And he's the source of all the wonderful things you enjoy (Ps. 16:11).

When you enjoy this breathtaking glory of God, you'll want other people to see it too! When you see a double rainbow in the sky or a flaming sunset, don't you automatically want to point it out to people near you? *Wow—look at that!* When you do this for God, you're glorifying him (Ps. 66:2; 96:3–8).

You're not making him more glorious, but you're recognizing how glorious he really is. He's more glorious than rainbows and sunsets. More than incredible rivers and animals. More than any part of your personality. More than anything you own. And more than any accomplishment or ability. God is more glorious than any of these things (Ps. 19:1; Isa. 40:12–13).

So why does God give us abilities or stuff or accomplishments? It's not to point to ourselves. Instead, God has given us life so we can point the spotlight to him—the true source of life (Matt. 5:16; 1 Pet. 2:9).

Eric Liddell knew that people enjoyed watching him run and watching him win. But he also knew that what they would enjoy most is God—the one who had made him fast.

That's the reason why, after running in Paris in 1924, Eric could walk away from an Olympic career. He could have run in 1928, but he wanted to point people to God in a different way, in a different place, even if it was hard and hidden from adoring fans.

Eric Liddell didn't run for his own glory. He ran—and served and loved and died—so people would see and enjoy a greater glory. He ran for the glory of God.

> So, whether you eat or drink, or whatever you do, do all to the glory of God. (1 Cor. 10:31)

Study Questions

Chapter 1: The Greatest Race

1. Describe Eric Liddell's 440-yard race at Stoke-on-Trent. What initially happened, and how did he react?

2. In what ways did Eric demonstrate his dedication and character both as an athlete and as a Christian?

Chapter 2: The Start

1. Describe Eric Liddell's parents and their background. What led them to China, and what kind of work were they involved in there?

2. What was the Boxer Rebellion? How did it start, and how did it impact China, espeically foreigners and missionaries?

3. How did Eric's parents and his childhood circumstances in China influence his character development?

Chapter 3: First Strides

1. After their return from China, where did the Liddell family travel and why?

2. Explain the Latin motto of Eltham College, *Gloria Filiorum Patres*, and how it was reflected in Eric's life.

3. How did Eric excel in sports at Eltham College, and what were some of his notable achievements in rugby, cricket, and running?

4. As Eric continued his education at the University of Edinburgh and participated in races, how did his running style and race times set him apart?

Chapter 4: In Training

1. How did Tom McKerchar's training methods differ from traditional coaching practices? How did he personally care for his athletes?

2. Detail Eric's dedication to training and the basics he learned under Tom McKerchar's coaching. What challenges did he face during training, and how did he overcome them?

Chapter 5: A New Course

1. Why did Eric agree to speak in Armadale, and what role did his faith in Christ play in his decision?

2. Describe Eric's experience when he spoke in Armadale about his faith and the transformation it sparked in his life.

3. How did Eric's speaking style and busy schedule reflect his personality and approach to serving God?

Chapter 6: Mounting Challenges

1. What dilemma did Eric face regarding the Olympic 100-meter race, and why did he refuse to compete? How did this decision affect his reputation?

2. What challenges did Eric face in preparing for the quarter-mile (400 meters) race instead of the 100-meter race?

3. Describe the mindset and determination Eric exhibited as he trained and prepared for the Olympics.

Chapter 7: Going for Gold

1. Describe Eric's experience during the 1924 Olympics in Paris, particularly focusing on his performance in the 200-meter and 400-meter races.

2. What was the public's response to Eric's Olympic victory? And how did Eric respond?

3. Explain the significance of Eric's statement, "My immortality comes from Christ—not a track and field stadium in France." How does this statement reflect his perspective on life and purpose?

Chapter 8: A Different Race

1. What was the political situation in China when Eric was preparing to travel there after the Olympics? How would that have affected life for foreigners in China at that time?

2. Describe Eric's teaching style and the impact he had on his students, both in and out of the classroom.

3. In what ways did Eric integrate his faith into his teaching and daily activities?

Chapter 9: Changing Lanes

1. What challenges and dangers were present in China during the years Eric taught at the Anglo-Chinese college?

2. Why did Eric decide to leave his teaching position and pursue pastoral work? What were the steps he took toward this decision, and what were its complications?

3. How would you describe Eric's relationship with Florence MacKenzie?

4. As you read about Eric's internal struggle between his commitment to his family's safety and his desire to help the suffering people of China—what aspect of that struggle resonated most with you?

Chapter 10: Running Risks

1. What were the challenges and dangers that Eric faced during his time in Siaochang, including his near misses with enemy soldiers and the escalating conflict?

2. During this conflict, how did Eric approach helping people? Which incident or detail was most striking to you? Why?

3. How did Eric's daily actions and interactions with the Smith family in Tientsin reflect his commitment to serving others and living according to Christ's example?

Chapter 11: To the Breaking Point

1. Describe the conditions of the Weihsien prison camp where Eric was held. How did these conditions impact daily life for the prisoners?

2. In what ways did Eric go above and beyond his own responsibilities? Provide specific examples of his actions and interactions with fellow prisoners.

3. How did Eric's daily devotion to God influence his interactions with others?

Chapter 12: The Final Lap

1. Explain the significance of the phrase "It is surrender"—Eric's final words. How does this phrase

reflect his outlook on life, his faith, and his relationship with God?

2. Compare and contrast how people from across the world remembered and honored Eric's life and legacy. Which one of their comments stood out most to you? Why?

3. How does Isaiah 40:31 (the verse that's partially included on the monument in his honor at Weihsien) encapsulate Eric's perseverance, his source of strength, and his unwavering faith?

4. Reflect on Eric's enduring legacy. How has his story continued to inspire people around the world, and what lessons can be learned from his life of service, faith, and determination?

Conclusion: Lessons from a Life

1. Explain the concept of "glory" as it relates to God and Eric's life. Discuss the ways in which Eric's life exemplified his commitment to living for the glory

of God. How did he use his athletic talents, achievements, and other aspects of his life to point people toward the greatness of God?

2. Reflect on the idea that God's glory is displayed in the beauty of creation, in his attributes, and in his unique identity as God. How should recognizing God's glory in these aspects of life transform our actions and attitudes?

3. Consider the statement that Eric didn't run for his own glory, but for the glory of God. How could focusing on glorifying God change the way you approach your talents, accomplishments, relationships, and even weaknesses?

Timeline

ERIC LIDDELL'S LIFE AND WORLD EVENTS

Year	Events	Age
1597	The sport of cricket is first recorded as having been played in the 1550s.	
1845	The sport of rugby is invented.	
1869	On November 17, the Suez Canal, connecting the Red Sea to the Mediterranean Sea, opens.	
1894	On July 25, the Japanese begin a war against China (the first Sino-Japanese War), which lasts until 1895.	
1898	James Dunlop Liddell travels from Scotland to become a missionary in northern China.	
1899	On October 18, the Boxer Rebellion begins in China and lasts for two years.	

ERIC LIDDELL'S LIFE　　WORLD EVENTS

Year	Events	Age
1899	On October 23, James Dunlop Liddell marries Mary Reddin in Shanghai, China.	
1900	On August 27, Eric's brother Robert ("Rob") Victor Liddell is born in Shanghai, China.	
1901	Queen Victoria of Great Britain dies. Italian Guglielmo Marconi sends first radio broadcast across the Atlantic Ocean.	
1902	On January 16, Eric Henry Liddell is born in Tientsin, China.	0
1903	On October 3, Eric's sister, Janet ("Jenny") Lillian Liddell, is born in Siaochang, China.	1
1903	On December 17, the Wright Brothers use their airplane to make the first controlled flight at Kitty Hawk, North Carolina (USA).	1
1907	Eric goes to Scotland to attend school at Eltham.	5
1909	On April 6, American Robert Peary is the first to reach the North Pole.	7
1911	On December 14, Norwegian Roald Amundsen is the first to reach the South Pole.	9
1912	On December 4, Eric's brother Ernest Blair Liddell is born in Beijing, China.	10
1914	On July 28, World War I begins. The Panama Canal opens on August 15. In September, C. S. Lewis (age 15) moves to Great Bookham (44 miles away from Eltham) to study with William Kirkpatrick.	12

Year	Events	Age
1918	Eric becomes captain of his school's rugby and cricket teams. He runs the 100-yard in 10.8 seconds.	16
1918	In February, a deadly Spanish Flu pandemic spreads around the world. On November 11, World War I ends.	16
1920	Eric begins attending the University of Edinburgh in Scotland. His major focus of study is called "Pure Science."	18
1921	Eric meets his trainer, Tom McKerchar and runs in his first season at Edinburgh University.	19
1921	July 23, the Chinese Communist Party is started.	19
1923	In March, Eric meets DP Thomson, and Eric starts speaking publicly about Jesus Christ in April. In July, Eric sets the British world record for the 100-yard race: 9.7 seconds.	21
1924	Summer Olympics held in Paris, France, from July 5–27.	22
1924	On July 8–11, Eric runs in the Olympics in Paris. He wins the gold medal for the 400-meter and the bronze for the 200-meter. On July 17, Eric graduates from Edinburgh University, and he begins to speak to crowds all over England and Scotland.	22
1925	In July, Eric leaves Scotland to teach at the Anglo-Chinese college.	23

Year	Events	Age
1926	Eric meets Florence Jean MacKenzie.	24
1927	On May 21, Charles Lindbergh completes the first nonstop flight across the Atlantic Ocean.	25
1928	Summer Olympics held in the Netherlands, July 28–August 12. (Eric declines to participate.) Walt Disney invents the character, Mickey Mouse.	26
1930	Eric runs his last competitive race, at the North China Championship, winning both the 100-meter and the 400-meter.	28
1931	On September 18, Japan invades China; this war ends in 1932. Widespread flooding in central China kills 4 million people.	29
1932	On June 22, Eric becomes a minister in the Scottish Congregational Church.	30
1933	On November 11, Eric's father, James Dunlop Liddell, dies in Drymen, Scotland.	31
1934	On March 27, Eric marries Florence MacKenzie in Tientsin, China.	32
1935	In July, Eric and Florence's first daughter, Patricia, is born.	33
1937	In January, Eric and Florence's second daughter, Heather, is born. In December, Eric and his brother Rob travel 400 miles from Tientsin to Saiochang, China.	35

Year	Events	Age
1937	On July 7, Japan invades China again; this war (the second Sino-Japanese War) lasts until 1945. In September, J. R. R. Tolkien publishes *The Hobbit*.	35
1938	Eric begins to serve as missionary pastor in Saiochang.	36
1938	In March, Adolf Hitler invades Austria and Czechoslovakia. The movie, *The Wizard of Oz*, is released in August.	36
1939	On September 1, World War II begins.	37
1941	The Japanese expel all foreigners from Saiochang. Eric returns to Tientsin and sends his wife and daughters to safety in Canada. In September, Eric and Florence's third daughter, Maureen, is born.	39
1941	On December 7, Japan bombs the United States navy fleet at Pearl Harbor, Hawaii. America enters World War II.	39
1942	In January, Eric continues to serve in Tientsin, lives with the Smith family, and writes *The Disciplines of the Christian Life*.	40
1942	In July, the first atomic bomb is created by the Manhattan Project.	40
1943	On March 30, the Japanese send Eric to a prison camp in Weihsien, China.	41
1944	Eric runs his final race, 220 yards, in the prison camp in Weihsien.	42

Year	Events	Age
1944	Eric's mother, Mary Reddin Liddell, dies on September 22 in Scotland.	42
1945	On February 21, Eric Liddell dies from a brain tumor.	43
1945	On May 7, Germany surrenders; the European portion of World War II ends. On September 2, Japan surrenders after atomic bombs are dropped on two Japanese cities, ending the Pacific portion of World War II.	
1949	In October, China becomes a Communist country under their leader, Mao Tse-Tung.	
1973	On May 30, Eric's older brother, Robert ("Rob") Victor Liddell, dies in Australia.	
1975	On February 11, Eric's younger brother, Ernest Blair Liddell, dies in Scotland.	
1981	On March 30, the movie about Eric Liddell's Olympic victory (*Chariots of Fire*) is released in theaters in Great Britain. Florence attends a showing and watches through tears.	
1984	On June 14, Eric's wife, Florence Jean MacKenzie, dies in Canada.	
1991	On June 9, the University of Edinburgh sets up a granite monument in memory of Eric, at the site of the former prison camp in Weifang.	
1994	On June 8, Eric's sister, Janet ("Jenny") Lillian Liddell Somerville, dies in Scotland.	

More to Explore

IF YOU'D LIKE TO READ MORE about Eric Liddell, there are several books that tell the story of his life. Some of the books in the list below are written for younger readers like you. Some of the adult books in the list are challenging to read but worth the effort.

BOOKS TO TRY NEXT

Janet and Geoff Benge. *Eric Liddell: Something Greater Than Gold.* YWAM, 1999. Part of a Christian biography series, this easy-to-read book (without any photographs) retells the story of Eric's entire life (199 pages).

John W. Keddie. *Eric Liddell: Finish the Race*. Trailblazer. Christian Focus, 2011. This chapter book (without photographs) is aimed at readers ages eight to fourteen, and was written by the same Christian author who wrote the longer book, *Running the Race* (160 pages).

ADULT BOOKS YOU MIGHT ENJOY

Eric T. Eichinger with Eva Marie Everson. *The Final Race: The Incredible World War II Story of the Olympian Who Inspired* Chariots of Fire. Tyndale, 2018. This well-written biography presents the story of Eric's life from a Christian perspective; it includes short fictionalized scenes at the start of each chapter and some beautiful full-color pages of photographs (304 pages).

Duncan Hamilton. *For the Glory: The Untold and Inspiring Story of Eric Liddell, Hero of* Chariots of Fire. Penguin Random House, 2017. Authored by an award-winning sportswriter, this brilliantly researched book includes many black-and-white photographs and is the most complete biography of Eric's life (400 pages).

John W. Keddie. ***Running the Race: Eric Liddell—Olympic Champion & Missionary.*** Christian Focus, 2020. Written from a Christian perspective and containing quite a few black-and-white photographs, this book covers all of Eric's life, but mainly focuses on all the details about his participation in sports (239 pages).

A Note on Sources

THE LANGUAGE in some quotations has been modernized. Also, while every effort has been made to ensure historical accuracy, some instances of dialogue in this biography represent creative reconstructions. Although such dialogue is not documented in the historical record, the author has sought to reflect the context, people, and available sources as accurately as possible.

The following books were used as sources in the research and writing of this biography.

Benge, Janet, and Geoff Benge. *Eric Liddell: Something Greater Than Gold.* YWAM, 1999.

Eichinger, Eric T., with Eva Marie Everson. ***The Final Race: The Incredible World War II Story of the Olympian Who Inspired*** **Chariots of Fire.** Tyndale, 2018.

Hamilton, Duncan. ***For the Glory: The Untold and Inspiring Story of Eric Liddell, Hero of*** **Chariots of Fire.** Penguin Random House, 2017.

Keddie, John W. ***Running the Race: Eric Liddell—Olympic Champion & Missionary*****.** Christian Focus, 2020.